Book 5
Wandering

The Promised Land

Written by Anne de Graaf
Illustrated by José Pérez Montero

Adventure Story Bible

Bible Society

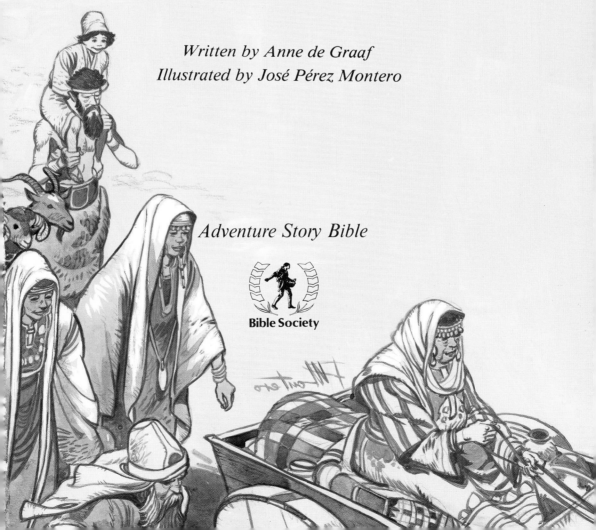

Wandering — The Promised Land

Contents — Numbers; Deuteronomy; Joshua 1—4

Book 5 — Bible Background

Moses was still leading the Israelites through the desert. They would spend many years wandering before they settled in the land that God had promised them.

The Book of Numbers in the Bible describes what happened during the long years in the desert. Numbers could be called "The Complaint Book", because it tells story after story of how the Israelites would not trust God to take care of them. Instead they grumbled, and were afraid.

The Book of Deuteronomy contains the speeches Moses gave his people, encouraging them to obey God. When the people did not obey God, again and again Moses asked God to forgive them. God did, but he did not lead them into the land he had promised them until forty years had passed.

Before Moses died he called his friend Joshua, and blessed him. Then Moses put his hand on Joshua, and Joshua took over leadership of the people of Israel. He led them into the land which God had promised them.

IN SEARCH OF A RICH AND FERTILE LAND

Life In the Desert

Numbers 9.15-23, 10.11-36

The Israelites were waiting to go to the land God promised them. God had a special way of showing them whether they should break camp. If they wanted to know, they would look over at God's tent.

Whenever God wanted the people to stop travelling and rest in one place, his cloud stayed over the special tent.

The cloud was a sign that God was with the camp. It rested just above the tent. As long as it stayed there, the Israelites stayed where they were. But if the people woke up one morning and saw the cloud had moved, they would pack up their belongings, load them on to the camels and donkeys, and break camp.

All the people could see the Lord's cloud, even the smallest child at the back.

During the two years when the people had camped at Sinai, they had learned from Moses how to follow all God's rules. Day after day passed, and weeks became months.

Every morning the people looked at God's tent to see if the cloud had moved. They wanted to go to the promised land, but God had not told them to travel yet. So they waited. While they waited, they grew strong and excited about the coming trip. They knew they were going to a wonderful place.

Finally, two years after they left Egypt, there came a day when the cloud moved out towards the desert.

"Today's the day!" the people called to each other. It was time to go. Family by family, they all set out. The first ones to leave the camp and lead the people were the priests, who carried the ark, or box, containing the pieces of stone with God's laws written on them.

The ark was the most precious thing the Israelites owned. The pieces of stone inside reminded them that they were God's chosen people. On them Moses had written down God's rules and promises for them.

After the ark came all the families. It was a huge crowd of people and animals. What a sight! There was so much dust! The nation of Israel was finally on its way to the land which God had promised to give them.

"It All Tastes the Same"

Numbers 11.1–9

No sooner had the people begun travelling in the desert than they forgot how much they had wanted to travel. They started to complain.

Their long rest at the camp by Mount Sinai made no difference. They did not like travelling. They did not like the dust and feeling unsettled. They did not like walking all day. They did not like moving their tents.

Most of all, though, they wanted meat. Their only food was the manna bread from heaven. They picked it up every day, ground it up, and made little cakes from it.

The problem was not that they were hungry. No, the Israelites had plenty to eat. But the people complained because they were tired of eating the same thing day after day after day, for every meal.

"We're sick of manna!" they cried out.

"If we have to eat another piece of manna, we'll die!" they grumbled. They were not at all thankful to have the food. All they could do was complain.

When God heard all the grumbling and saw no one saying "thank you" for their food any more, he grew angry. His anger overflowed into a fire on the edge of the camp. The people screamed. Smoke was everywhere. Many tents were burnt down.

But still, the people did not learn to be thankful for what they had. "Give us meat!" they shouted at Moses.

"We would rather be slaves in Egypt," they said. "At least there we had fresh fish and fruit and vegetables."

"We want our cucumbers!"

"We want onions and garlic!"

"We want meat!"

Meat and More Meat

Numbers 11.10–35

Moses was very frustrated that the Israelites had forgotten so soon that God had promised to take care of them.

"Are these people like little babies, who cannot learn?" he asked God. "Why am I the one who is stuck with these spoilt children?" Moses felt very tired and very old. He did not even like the Israelites any more.

Time and time again they had broken promises and given up, without even trying. Now they were making a great fuss about their food, not even thinking how good it was to be alive and free. God was angry with them, too. But God knew the people's grumbling was not Moses' fault.

6

Because God did not want Moses to carry the heavy burden of a weak people he said, "Moses, choose seventy of the leaders of the Israelites. Bring them to the special tent, and I will take some of the spirit I have given to you, and give it to them. Then they can do things for you, and you will not feel so tired. You will have helpers."

God told Moses he would teach the Israelites a lesson. "I will send them meat. But I will send them more meat than they know what to do with. And they will grow so sick of it, they will never cry out for meat again. They will have to eat it until it comes out of their ears."

So he sent a huge flock of quails to settle on both sides of the camp. The people spent days gathering all the birds. They ate and ate until they all had stomach aches. Then they ate some more. Many became very sick.

God became angry with the people and caused an epidemic to break out among them, so that many died.

This happened because the people forgot how God had taken care of them, and complained that they should never have left Egypt.

Moses Is Challenged by His Two Best Friends

Numbers 12.1–16

Moses had two very good friends. They were his brother Aaron, who had helped him lead the people out of Egypt, and his sister Miriam, who had watched over him so well when he was a baby.

Although both Aaron and Miriam had cared for Moses, as the journey through the desert wore on, they began to criticize Moses. They, too, had been close to God at times, and they wondered why Moses was always the leader. "Why can't we lead the Israelites sometimes?" they asked themselves.

God heard what Aaron and Miriam were saying, and he was not happy. Moses was a very good man. He did not really want to be the leader. Over and over again he had asked

God to take the leadership away from him. Moses never did feel he was the right man for the job.

God called Aaron and Miriam to come with Moses to his special tent. The cloud came down over the tent and God told Aaron and Miriam that they should not speak against Moses. Then, when the cloud lifted off the tent, Miriam had a terrible surprise.

She looked down at her hands and was horrified to see that her skin was all white and flaky. She was very, very ill.

Moses did not want his sister to be ill, so he called to God, "Please heal her. Do not let her stay like this." God listened to Moses, but said that Miriam must live apart from the people for a week.

When a week was over, Miriam was able to come back and join the camp again. From then on Miriam and Aaron did not question God's choice for a leader. They tried their hardest to help Moses in all the ways they could.

ON THE BORDER
Within Sight of the Promised Land

Numbers 13.1–30

As the people moved through the desert there came a day when God said to Moses, "Send spies into the country I am planning to give you. Get them to see what sort of land it is and what the people are like who live there."

Moses did as God asked. He chose one man from each of the twelve tribes of Israel. These tribes came from Joseph and his eleven brothers, the sons of Jacob. The twelve men left the camp, and the Israelites waited for them.

After many, many days the men returned. Amongst them were Caleb, from the tribe of Judah, and Joshua, whom God had blessed as a general. They said to Moses, "Oh yes! You should see the land. It is so beautiful, with strong trees, and gentle hills. Flowers bloom everywhere and the crops of the people there are rich and plentiful. It really is as God promised, a rich and fertile land."

There was only one problem, though. The people who lived on the land were all very good fighters. Joshua and Caleb knew that with God on their side they could drive those people out of the land. Joshua remembered how God had given them victory in the past.

"We Are Not Strong Enough"

Numbers 13.31–14.12; Deuteronomy 1.19–33

The other men who had spied out the land with Joshua and Caleb were not so sure the people living in the promised land could be defeated. They were afraid, and they were troublemakers. They lied to the people. "Oh no, you would never want to live there," they said. "It's a terrible land; the sort of place where you would always be hungry and thirsty, and no matter how hard you worked, crops would never grow."

The people believed these other men. They could have believed God's promises, but instead they believed these men who were not brave. "Oh Moses," they cried, "what have you done to us?"

Moses groaned. The people were complaining again.

"Moses, we want to go back to Egypt!"

"Moses, we do not want our wives and children to be taken prisoner by these tribes who are stronger than we are. We would be better off as slaves."

"Moses, it was all your idea to leave Egypt in the first place. We should never have listened to you."

Moses and Aaron bowed to the ground in front of all the people, and Joshua and Caleb tore their clothes in sorrow. They assured the Israelites that the land they had explored was an excellent land.

They begged the people to be reasonable and remember the promises of God. But the people would not listen. They were very stubborn and liked feeling sorry for themselves.

The people were so upset, they threatened to throw rocks at them and kill them. But suddenly they saw the dazzling light of the Lord's presence appear over the tent.

The Lord said to Moses, "What is wrong with these people that again and again they do not believe me? I cannot put up with them much longer. I will destroy them and keep you alive, and we will start again."

The Forty Year Punishment

Numbers 14.13–45; Deuteronomy 1.34–45

When Moses heard God say he would destroy the Israelites, he pleaded with God. "No, Lord, please do not kill them all. What would the Egyptians say? You worked so many miracles to help us escape from Egypt. And for what? To kill us out in the desert? No, you would not want the Egyptians to say that you killed your people in the desert because you were not able to bring them into the land you promised to give them. Please forgive them."

Once again, God forgave the people. But because they were stubborn and had refused so many times to believe God and trust him, God said that no one over twenty years of age would set foot in the promised land.

"These people must wander in the desert," he said. "All of them over twenty will die out here, except for Caleb and Joshua, who believed in me. Instead of bringing them into the land soon, as I could have — for you are close by — the people will wander in the desert for forty years. They will die in the desert, and their children will be the ones finally to settle in the land."

When the people heard this, they cried out loud. But it was too late. God had made up his mind.

Despite God's punishment, the people decided that if the land was so close, they should go to it right away. They paid no attention to Moses' warnings. They collected all their weapons saying, "God will help us

win against these other tribes." They ignored the fact that God had just said they would not be the ones to drive the tribes away.

The people went off to battle even though Moses and the ark stayed in the camp.

When the people returned, they had lost. Many men had died in a battle which God had not helped them win.

For the next thirty-eight years the Israelites wandered from place to place. The Lord did not stop leading them, but neither did he lead them straight to the promised land. Their punishment was real. They must spend the rest of their lives walking in circles, close to Canaan, but never able to enter it.

A STUBBORN PEOPLE
Moses Loses His Patience

Numbers 20.2-11

Year after year went by until nearly forty years had passed since the people had left Egypt. In all that time they went nowhere, slowly. They moved from camp to camp. All the adults who had left Egypt were old now. Their children had become adults, and some had children of their own. But in all that time, the people still had not learned to stop complaining.

"Moses, we're thirsty!"

"Moses, it's too hot! Where can we find water?"

The cries for water could be heard all round the Israelite camp.

"The people are complaining again," Aaron said to his brother. Moses was very old by then. He said nothing. He made a sign for Aaron to follow him. Together the two men went to God's tent, which housed the ark, the box containing the ten commandments.

Moses called on the Lord, asking where they should find water. The Lord told Moses to take his stick and speak to a nearby rock. Then there would be enough water for everybody.

So Moses took his stick and he and Aaron went to the rock.

"Why did you lead us out here?" the people yelled at them. They still had not learned that God took care of them.

Then Moses got angry. They were like babies, each one of them. "Here, you want water?" he called to them. "We'll give you water!" Moses raised his stick and hit the rock twice with it. Water came gushing out. There was enough water for all the people and their sheep and cattle, donkeys and camels.

But Moses and Aaron had made a mistake. When Moses gave the water to the people, he did not tell the people that it was God's power bringing the water. He had lost his patience, shouted, and hit the rock.

Moses and Aaron Are Punished

Numbers 20.12-13, 22-29

God was angry with Moses and Aaron. He said, "Because you did not tell the people the water was from me, you will not set foot in the promised land, either."

Later, when the Israelites had travelled to the foot of yet another mountain, God told Moses to bring Aaron and Aaron's son up to the top of the mountain.

God said that it was time for Aaron to die. He would not see the promised land.

God made Aaron's son the head priest. When Moses and Aaron's son came down the mountain and the people realized that their priest was dead, they were very sad. They tore their clothes and wailed, grieving for a whole month.

14

They missed Aaron now that he was dead. Yet, when he was alive, they had not paid any attention to him and often ignored his warnings. Now that he had gone, they wanted Aaron back.

But Moses was the one who missed Aaron the most. Aaron had been Moses' big brother, his helper. Together he and Aaron had disciplined the people, and again and again pleaded with God to forgive the Israelites each time they were bad. Nobody grieved for Aaron more than Moses.

War and Settlement of a Part of Israel

Deuteronomy 2.26–3.29

When the forty years of wandering were almost over, most of the people who had been in Egypt were dead. It would soon be time for God to lead their children, now the adults and new leaders of Israel, into the promised land.

As the Israelites passed through other tribes' territories, they were often attacked. The tribes saw all the animals the Israelites had with them and they thought, "We would like all those sheep and cattle for ourselves."

But the Lord kept his promise, and showed Moses and Joshua how to defeat these enemy tribes. Time and time again the Israelites won the battles. Finally they owned whole cities in which the women and children could live. The Israelite men went out and fought war after war. Slowly but surely they defeated the tribes living near the land that God had promised them.

Moses and Joshua were the leaders of the Israelites. Joshua and Caleb had been faithful to God so many years ago, when they first spied out the promised land. So God said that they would be the only adults from the group who had left Egypt to go and live there.

Moses told Joshua, "Remember that God is with you. Remember how he has helped us win all these battles."

Then Moses fell on to his knees to pray. He pleaded with the Lord, asking him to let him see the promised land. Moses remembered that many years before, he had hit the rock to get water, and had not told the people that the water coming from the rock was from God. So God had said he would not allow Moses to go into the promised land. But Moses longed to see the new land.

Finally God told Moses he would see the land before he died. "You will see the land," he said, "but you may not set foot in it."

Moses did not argue. He had learned, after so many years of following God, that it was better to obey. God had better things planned than even Moses could have imagined.

Balaam Knows Best

Numbers 22.1–14

As the Israelites fought tribe after tribe, they came closer and closer to the land by the River Jordan. Everyone they fought against they defeated, for God had made Joshua think like a great general.

Eventually the Israelites came near the land of Moab. The king of Moab was called Balak.

He saw how many Israelites there were and already knew they hardly ever lost a battle. He sent for a man called Balaam, who was like a wizard. The king thought to himself, "If I can get Balaam to put a curse on the Israelites, the bad things will come true and I can defeat them."

Balaam came from Moab. He was not an Israelite. Yet he had heard that there was one God greater than all the others and he believed in that one God. Before he predicted what would happen, he always tried to find out what the one God wanted.

When Balaam heard that Balak wanted to see him because he wanted him to curse the Israelites, Balaam told the king's messengers, "Spend the night here, and tomorrow I will tell you what the Lord says to me."

God told Balaam not to go with these men or curse the Israelites, because they were God's chosen people.

The next morning Balaam told the messengers what God had said, and sent them on their way.

The Talking Donkey

Numbers 22.15–24.25

When the king's messengers told Balak that Balaam stood up for the Israelites, the king sent more important messengers to ask him to come and curse the Israelites. He offered him a big reward for coming. But Balaam said, "Even if Balak offered me all the silver and gold in the palace, I would never disobey God. But please stay the night as the others did, and I will see if God has something else to tell me."

That night God told Balaam to get ready to go with the messengers. "But only do what I tell you," God said.

So the next morning Balaam got on his donkey and rode back with the messengers. But on the way, his old, reliable donkey acted strangely. Instead of walking down the road, she ran off into a field. Balaam hit her.

The donkey carried on, but as she reached a narrow part of the road, she squeezed up against the wall, crushing Balaam's foot. Again Balaam hit her hard.

When he tried to get her to move on, the donkey lay down in the road. Balaam lost his temper with the donkey, and hit her again.

Then the Lord gave the donkey the power to speak. "Why do you hit me?" she said.

Balaam said, "Why are you suddenly so stubborn?"

"Haven't I always done what you wanted and taken care we were never harmed?" the donkey asked. Balaam nodded.

Then the Lord opened Balaam's eyes, and he saw the angel of the Lord standing in the middle of the road, holding a sword. Balaam threw himself on the ground.

"Why have you hit your donkey three times?" the angel asked. "If it had not been for her, you would have been dead by now. For I was ready to kill you if you had tried to get past me."

Balaam was sorry, and asked what he should do. "Do you want me to turn back?" he asked.

"No," the angel answered. "But make sure you say only what the Lord tells you to say when you see the king of Moab."

Balaam agreed.

When Balaam reached the king, the king asked him to curse Israel, and promise they would lose. But Balaam said, "These are a great people. They are God's chosen people. If God wants them to win, they will win."

Then Balak was angry because he knew there was no way that his Moabite soldiers could ever defeat the Israelites. The Israelites had God on their side.

MOSES INSPIRES GOD'S PEOPLE
Teach Your Children About God

Deuteronomy 6.1–25

God was still preparing his people to go into their new land. He told the Israelites to make sure that their children knew about God. The Lord did not want the Israelites ever to forget how God had taken them out of Egypt and rescued them.

"When you are settled in your land," he told them, "remember not to worship any other god but me. I am your Lord. Always remember the miracles I have performed for you."

It was very important for the Israelites to remember what God had done for them. The people did not have any of the stories of God and the Israelites written down, as they are now, in the Bible. Instead, they learned the rules of God because Moses had taught them. They learned from their leaders.

The children did not go to school then. They were taught by their parents. So it was especially important that the parents told the children all the stories about God.

"As the children get older," God said, "make sure they hear all about your life in Egypt, and how I saved you.

"Talk to the children when you sit in your house and when you go for a walk. Tell them again and again what happened, when you are resting, and when you are working," God said.

The children of Israel were taught by their parents always to say "thank you" to God. They learned about all the rules God had given Moses. They learned how important it was to trust God and believe that he loved them.

The Choice of Life or Death

Deuteronomy 29.1—30.20; 31.2

Moses knew he would not lead the Israelites
for much longer, so he called together all the
people of Israel and said in a loud voice, "You
have a choice!" The people shook their heads.
What was Moses talking about? "All of you
who want to live, raise your hands!"

The crowd mumbled, "What does he
mean?"

"Of course we want to live!" they thought.

"Yes, yes!" they called. So all the people
raised their hands.

"All those who want to die, raise your
hands!" Moses called out.

The crowd quickly lowered their hands. A
silence fell over them and they waited. No
hands were raised. The people waited to hear
what Moses would say.

"Today," he shouted, "you have said you
choose life, not death. God wants to make a
promise to you. He wants to give you food
and water, a beautiful land, and large flocks.

This is life. He wants to give you peace. He
will give you all these things if you obey his
laws.

"But if you do things on your own, if you
are proud, if you forget the great things God
did to save you from slavery in Egypt, then
you will die!" Moses paused.

"No! It will be worse than death. This land
will burn and everything will be ruined. People
will look at you and say, 'It is a terrible thing
that has happened to the Israelites.' Do you
believe me?"

"Yes, Moses, we will obey!" the people
shouted back.

Moses' Last Song

Deuteronomy 31.1—34.7

Moses was one hundred and twenty years old. Before he died, God asked him to write down a song to teach the Israelites.

Moses wrote this song so the people could sing it around their camp and cooking fires. He wanted them to teach it to their children and he wanted the women to hum it whenever they were doing their chores.

Moses' song was all about the love of God. It told how faithful God had been through the years, and how powerful he was. It also told of how weak and disobedient the people had been. God wanted the Israelites to know the song well, so that it would remind them of these things.

When Moses had finished singing, he felt very tired. Moses wanted so badly to see the land he had searched for during the last forty years. He asked God if the time had come.

"Yes," the Lord said, "you can see the land now, but you will not go into it. Joshua will lead the people into the land."

So Moses called Joshua to him and said, "You must be very brave and strong. You are the one who will lead these people when they occupy the land that the Lord promised them. The Lord himself will lead you. He will never leave you. Do not lose courage or be afraid."

God told Moses, "Go up Mount Nebo and from there you will see the land of Canaan." When Moses reached the top, he looked across the River Jordan to the promised land. He stood on the hill and stared, his eyes drinking in the sight of God's land.

Moses said, "Thank you, Lord." In some ways, it was enough just to see the land.

While Moses was gazing out at the land which would soon belong to his people, he died. He died a strong man, still able to see and think clearly. He had been Israel's greatest leader, someone who was specially close to God.

GOD'S GENERAL
The New Leader

Deuteronomy 34.9; Joshua 1.1–18

When the Lord spoke to Joshua after Moses' death, he said three times, "Be strong and brave!"

"Be strong and brave! Joshua, you will bring all these people into the promised land, Canaan. You will have to fight more wars, but I will help you win," God said. "Be strong and brave, obey my laws, and the Lord your God will be with you wherever you go. Be strong and brave!"

Joshua told the leaders to go through the camp giving good news to all the people. A cry went up throughout the huge camp, "Three more days!"

"What?" The people turned from their jobs, their cooking, and taking care of their animals. "What's that?"

"In three more days we will cross the River Jordan and enter the promised land! Three more days!"

After forty long years of walking through the desert, they would finally see the land God had promised to Abraham, Isaac, Jacob, Joseph, and all their great-grandfathers so long ago.

When their leaders went to Joshua to find out more, Joshua told them they must all work together to help fight off the enemy tribes in the new land.

"We will do all that you tell us, Joshua," they promised, "and may God be with you as he was with Moses." They were very thankful to God that they would finally enter the promised land.

"I Spy the Enemy"

Joshua 2.1-7

Joshua stood before two of his men. They were his best soldiers, brave and clever. "I have a secret mission for you," he said.

The two men watched their general Joshua. Their dark eyes danced with excitement. They were especially good at secret missions.

"I want you to sneak into the land ahead of us, into the city of Jericho, and find out how strong it is. Find out if the people are ready to fight us, how many soldiers they have, what types of weapons there are — are they bronze or iron? Then come back and tell me. After we cross the River Jordan, your information will help us take the city of Jericho."

The men nodded and looked at each other. It was just the type of mission they liked best.

That afternoon the two men slipped silently into the city. It was surrounded by great thick walls. At night the gates were closed tight and guards patrolled the tops of the walls, making sure no one entered or left.

When they were in the city, they started to look for somewhere to stay the night.

They hurried down the alley-ways because it seemed that they had aroused the suspicion of the people in the city, and found a place to stay with Rahab, who was a prostitute.

Word reached the king of Jericho that some Israelites had come that night to spy out the country, so he sent word to Rahab, "The men in your house have come to spy out the whole country! Bring them out!"

"Some men did come to my house," she answered, "but I don't know where they were from. They left at sunset before the city gate was closed. I didn't find out where they were going, but if you chase after them quickly, you can catch them."

The king's men left the city in hot pursuit, and the city gate was shut behind them.

24

The Spies Escape

Joshua 2.6-14

Rahab smiled to herself and went up on to
the roof where, just before the guards had
come, she had hidden the men. The two men
climbed out of their hiding place.

"I know all about you Israelites," she said to
them. "God is on your side. He blesses
whatever you do. You have won all the wars
around here and all the men in Jericho are
scared to fight you.

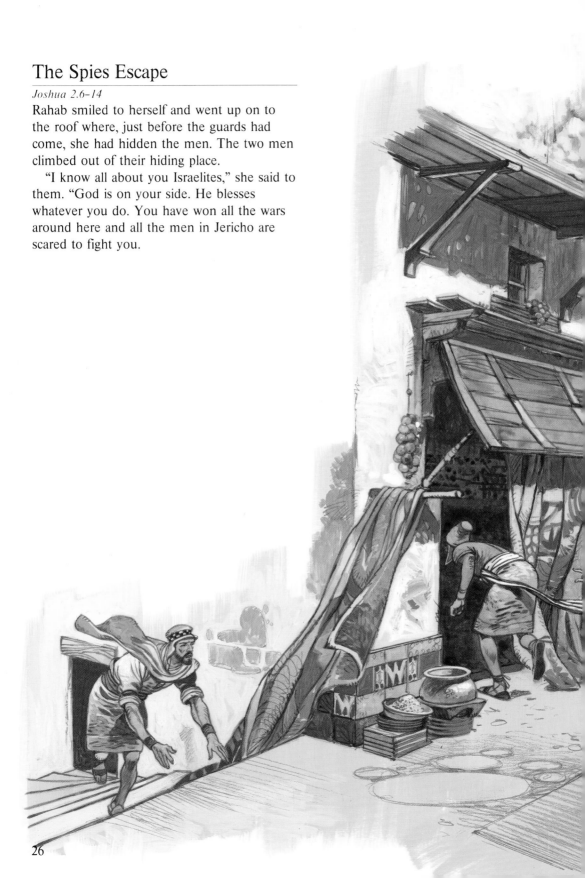

"If I help you escape, will you remember me and my family, and not harm us when you conquer Jericho?"

"You save our lives, and we will save yours," the men replied. "Yes, we will save you and your family if you help us get out of here."

The woman nodded. Then she motioned for them to follow her. And suddenly she disappeared up another set of stairs they had not seen when they first entered the house.

Saved By a Rope

Joshua 2.15-21

The men climbed the narrow steps until they
found themselves in a tiny room with a low
roof. They could barely stand upright without
bumping their heads. A small window was the
only light.

"See, this is how you will escape," Rahab
said. She motioned to the window. One of the
spies went to look out of it. He saw that the
side of the house was actually part of the wall
surrounding Jericho.

Rahab gave him some rope. "If you climb
out here, you will be on the outside of the
city. Go into the hills and the guards will not
find you. Stay hidden for three days."

The man took the rope from her. "Rahab,
the only way we can pay you back for helping
us to escape is if you tie some red cord to this
window. Then when we conquer Jericho,
everyone who stays inside your house will be
safe."

The other spy came forward. "But, if you
betray us," he said in a low voice, "and we are
caught, you can expect no mercy from the
Israelites."

She nodded. The men opened the window,
poked their heads out to make sure the way
was clear, and fastened the rope to a pillar.
Slowly they lowered themselves out of the
house and down the wall, bouncing against it
with their feet.

When they reached the ground and no
alarm was sounded, they disappeared into the
darkness.

Rahab pulled the rope back inside, and tied
the red cord to the window. She knew it was
her ticket to safety. For if God wanted the
Israelites to capture Jericho, then they surely
would.

On the Edge of the Promised Land

Joshua 2.22–3.13

The spies from Israel hid for three days. When they knew the woman had not betrayed them and they were safe, they ran back to the Israelite camp and reported to Joshua.

"There is no doubt about it, Joshua," the men said. "God has gone before us and struck terror into the hearts of our enemies. The woman who helped us escape said all the men in Jericho were afraid of us already."

"The city is practically ours."

"We will invade Jericho in a few days' time," Joshua said. "Today, though, is the day for which we have waited so long."

At first his soldiers did not understand what he meant. Then a huge grin stretched itself across Joshua's bearded face. "Today is the day the Lord will lead us into the promised land!" The men took up the call and ran to the other leaders throughout the camp to pass on the news. Soon it spread from one end to the other, "Today is the day!"

The people were so excited. They had hoped for this day, and counted down the days, but they had been almost afraid it would never come. "Today is the day," they told each other, laughing and shouting for joy.

They had packed all their tents and were ready for the final stage of their journey. The river flowed in front of their camp. On the other side of the River Jordan was the land of Canaan, the land God had promised them.

The River Jordan was flooding at that time of year. All the snow in the hills had melted, and so much water poured down the river that it was overflowing. How would the Israelites ever cross?

Crossing the River Jordan

Joshua 3.14–4.24

God gave Joshua special instructions to give to the priests. They were to carry the ark containing the ten commandments into the water.

The priests looked at the fast-moving waves and shook their heads, but they obeyed. As soon as the priests' toes touched the water, the waves piled up, just as the Red Sea had done for Moses, when their parents and grandparents had escaped from Egypt. A dry path stretched before the priests who carried the ark.

They walked into the middle of the river bed. It was perfectly dry! Then Joshua called the people to follow. They all walked around the priests who held the ark, and crossed the River Jordan.

When all the Israelites had passed by the priests into the new land and were on the other side of the river, Joshua looked down from the hill where he had been watching everything. He remembered the promise of God to Abraham, the first leader of their people.

God had said, "I will make you into a great nation, and you will number more than all the stars in the sky, and this land of Canaan will belong to you."

There Joshua saw stretching before him countless people, all Israelites, all members of Abraham's family. After nearly five hundred years, Abraham's children had come home to Canaan, their promised land.

God told Joshua to choose twelve men to take twelve stones from the place where the priests stood with the ark. When they had done this, the Lord told Joshua to command the priests carrying the ark to come out of the Jordan. When they reached the river bank, the waters crashed back into place.

The people then set up camp, and Joshua set up the stones as a reminder of the time and place when God brought his people to Canaan and made the waters of the River Jordan dry up.

Joshua called out in a loud voice, "In future, when your children ask what these stones mean, you will tell them of the time when Israel crossed the Jordan on dry ground. Because of this all the people on earth will know that our God is powerful, and that we should always respect and obey him."

The people broke into a loud cheer. At that moment they loved God and wanted to follow God's chosen leader, Joshua. The people of Israel had come back to the land of Canaan, the land that God had promised them. Their long years of wandering were over.

Adventure Story Bible   Old Testament